# Incarnations of the Heart

# Incarnations of the Heart

Poems and Prose Out of History

MARK S. MCLEOD-HARRISON

WIPF & STOCK · Eugene, Oregon

INCARNATIONS OF THE HEART
Poems and Prose Out of History

Copyright © 2013 Mark S. McLeod-Harrison. All rights reserved. Except for brief quotations in critical publications or reviews, no part of this book may be reproduced in any manner without prior written permission from the publisher. Write: Permissions. Wipf and Stock Publishers, 199 W. 8th Ave., Suite 3, Eugene, OR 97401.

Wipf & Stock
An Imprint of Wipf and Stock Publishers
199 W. 8th Ave., Suite 3
Eugene, OR 97401

www.wipfandstock.com

ISBN 13: 978-1-62564-145-8

Manufactured in the U.S.A.

"Mother and Son" and "Episodes on the Eve of War" appeared first in *The Rolling Coulter*, "The Fundamentalist" in *The Reformed Journal*" and "Creases and Furrows" in *TapJoe*. Copyright was retained by the author.

I dedicate this book to one who can no longer read it,
one who would now find it too challenging to read,
and one who will read it
and have a cry and a laugh or two.
In memory of Granny B.
(who fully entered the communion of saints at 93)
and for my Grannie at 101
(go, Grannie, go)
and my 80-year-old Mom
(who will be reading when she's 100).

The women in my family have great longevity genes.
At 57, I'm hoping I got them too.

# Contents

*Foreword* | ix
*Preface* | xi

As if that were a comfort | 1
An Incarnation Not So Far Away | 2
Mother and Son | 5
The Word | 6
Nail, Nail | 9
Father and Sons | 10
Mother Made Life | 12
Enchanted Rock | 16
Down on all Fours | 17
Communion of the Saints | 18
The Muse | 20
The Teacher | 21
The Teacher Again | 22
A commentary on the low flight of birds | 23
Creases and Furrows | 25
The Fundamentalist | 26
Suits | 28
Rigor Mortis | 30
Long Time Down to Death | 31
Episodes on the Eve of War: January 14, 1991 | 36

Messiah | 39

Unless a seed dies | 42

As much about me as Joey | 44

The Third Day | 50

Take a Little Water | 54

Euhemerists | 59

The Philosopher's Hill | 60

Advent Meditation on Ecclesiastes | 62

Time | 63

The Farm Photograph | 65

Pioneer Settlement in Muskoka: An Agri/Cultural History | 67

In Anselm's Cave | 69

Scything with Friends | 71

Mortar and Pestle | 73

Advent in San Antonio | 81

How Old Was My Granddad? | 83

A Plant Too Quick | 86

Ludwig's Language Games | 87

The Anti-Hum Society | 90

Christological Hand Flappings: On Being an Autistic Child with Autism | 96

# Foreword

A book of poems, by a philosopher? Dull reading... perhaps. Yet poetry and philosophy, for all their ancient debate, have much in common. Both are after the mystery. In my book *Apologizing for God: The Importance of Living in History* (Cascade Books 2011) I presented the centrality of history to developing a good philosophy. One's position in history is essential to understanding not just philosophy but the Christian faith. The Christian faith, as life lived in history, is an antidote to the extremes of relativism and cold objectivity, of postmodernism and modernism. (Please don't let those terms put off the potential reader of this book. I promise not to use them again.) That book could be called autobiographical philosophy or even storied philosophy. I say there that autobiography is largely biography. Much of its point depended on things I'd learned along the way from various people. This book continues that theme but with a slightly different approach, viz., poetry and a few short essays and creative nonfiction.

Another way of thinking can frame this work, however. Many years ago, I was introduced by my Catholic, Orthodox and Anglican friends to the notion of the communion of the saints. The doctrine has become central to my understanding of the Christian faith and our history with God. While I've tried in other venues to write something philosophically cogent about the doctrine, I've had little success. The communion is easier to see, hear, taste, smell or feel than to write about philosophically. Sometimes, indeed, the veil between this world and the next is lowered and the kingdom of heaven with all its saints can be seen directly. At least, that's been my experience. I can feel the communion all around me, at least on my good days.

## Incarnations of the Heart

I've learned that the communion of the saints is the result of God's deepest love for us. Indeed, when more fully understood, the communion *is* God's deepest love for us. The poems and essays included here are the result of experiencing that love. Unfortunately, they do the communion poor justice. I apologize for getting things wrong when I have. But more importantly, I apologize for not getting the beauty of the communion portrayed in anything like its full glory.

Many people have pointed me toward the communion simply by being members of it. In fact, there's no way to write enough books or even poems and essays to honor every individual who has had an incarnate heart in helping me see God. Many of you know who you are, but perhaps many others don't—you've been lovers incognito, even to yourselves. But in the end, God not only knows who you are but God celebrates your lives. So do I celebrate your lives. But more importantly, the Holy Three will someday, if it hasn't happened already, welcome you fully into the perichoresis—the divine dance—that is God's love for all of us.

We are the second incarnations of God. As the body of Christ, we are the communion of the saints. As such, our names are written in the Lamb's book of life and because of that, perhaps I can be forgiven for not listing everyone who has had a hand and a heart in helping me know God better.

# Preface

For hundreds of years, art of all sorts has been supported by the gifts of people other than the artists. This, too, is part of the communion of the saints and many of those saints remain hidden. When the gifts are anonymous, someone arranges for that support to be distributed. In this case, the distribution came through George Fox University. I thank Patrick Allen (retiring provost) and Linda Samek (interim provost), for scraping the bottom of the 2012–2013 funding barrel to arrange the finances enabling this collection to be published. And Patrick, you've been, as a philosopher/poet might say: the-best-of-all-possible provosts. Thank you.

# As if that were a comfort

*For Susan*

Angels never appear
without warning:
"Do not be afraid,
the Lord is with you."

As if that were a comfort,
since God is scarier than
angels.

Babies never appear
without a warning either.
"Do not be afraid,
the Lord is with you."

As if that were a comfort,
since babies are scarier than
God.

God, at least, doesn't need
    a change of diapers,
        the right amount of milk,
    a hand to hold, and

God never turns into a
    teenager.

# An Incarnation Not So Far Away

*For Susan,*
*Christmas 2007*

The incarnation
this year
seems
a celebration
of a
far off
deity.

Except for Micah dancing,
arms waving,
face smiling as he
sounds out
the whirring of blenders
and humming of vacuums.

Before he was born,
I was caught up with the
infinite potentials
of children growing
beautiful and strong.
I'd forgotten how infinities hide in
diapers, broken teeth,
and sleepless nights.

I can hear the floor above me creaking.
You are walking,
walking toward

sweet sleep
down some very long road knowing
even as Micah sleeps
that you will lie awake
thinking of tomorrows and
yesterdays, of friends and hopes,
of clients and a husband who oft
times doesn't know how to
love.

Mary pondered these things
in her heart as she lay awake,
Joseph no doubt sleeping.


Oh, he had two dreams that woke him up,
one told him to love Mary,
another to fear Herod.

Like me, his feelings were often lost,
shadowed among thoughts of buildings and money,
of how things will be tomorrow,
just out of reach to his competence.
We men are so adolescent,
growth stunted at fifteen,
one feeling masquerading as another.

Not knowing how to love,
we must be awoken by dreams sent by
angels. It is we men who need to be
saved through childbirth.

Our own. Such births come,
but only through women.

So even if this year the

incarnation seems a celebration of
a far-off God, remember that the
angels won't abandon us, so
don't be afraid. There is still an incarnation.
This year Jesus came
alive before Christmas
when he turned to
wink at his male followers too
thick to see the hope.
This year Jesus laughed
when the woman argued,
supplying a theological
zinger and won.
This year the children
showed up the dads
and led them to the
already-not-yet.
This year Jesus made a
glorious comeback
as a lover of women and
they will be healed.

But not women alone.

For this year,
this year,
Jesus came off
the pages
of your heart and
into mine,

an incarnation not so far away.

# Mother and Son

The blood came earlier than they had dreamed.
A woman newly made, she married.
Her broken water buoyed her thoughts,
the blood baptized and the water washed.

The blood came earlier than they had dreamed.
One man newly made, he died.
His broken body buoyed her thoughts,
the blood baptized and the water washed.

# The Word

The most amazing thing of all
was the Word
who could not speak, the Word
who shaped the world
dropping down
through the legs of a woman
a sure surprise for her,
this wondrous one
whose father had no flesh.

The Word who now for eternity
was shaped by the world
he couldn't speak about.
The Word made flesh,
a comprehension beyond even
him, left speechless,
God gripping for reality
he hadn't lived.
The Word beyond words,
beyond metaphor,
beyond propositions,
beyond language.
The Word appears and makes
his tent among us, gathering food,
lighting fires, walking among sheep,
picking up splinters foreshadowing
a deeper pain.

This Word writ large among us, yet

hidden in the brambles of philosophy,
our fragile attempts to drag heaven down.
This Word calls us to stop if only
for a moment to breathe the Spirit of his
heart, to lick up dew he leaves each
night, to open our eyes and see,
the second Adam, forever enfleshed,
not merely in some body
belonging to him, but in
our flesh too, forever human,
forever brother, one by choice,
not forced to love.

This incarnate God
who would have come
with tabernacles,
bread and wine
even if had we not sinned,
wanting only to be with us, near to ones
for whom his romance is far
greater than any we can grasp.

This incarnate God is one
to whom we at last will speak
in quiet tones, lovers who understand
the other's needs.
We take his cup now,
knowing that in drinking deep
our very souls are altered.
The bread too, dry and without taste,
yet made in kitchens served by angels,
will suffice, a transfiguration we can only glimpse
among us now. Tell no one,
the whisper comes.

In our delight to hear the Word,

we shout from housetops simple tales
of how he came among us.
And yet we know,
this Word,
this body,
this truth is one we cannot finally speak, but
only live and therein we are
changed.

# Nail, Nail

*For Ian*

The boy had a penchant for nails.
His father didn't use them much.
Iron was expensive,
so corners were fit
without, whenever the cost
was too great.

The child threw his hands in the air,
laughing and crying "nail, nail"
when he'd hear the hammer do its work
and a nail was needed by his father.

The man had a penchant for nails.
His father didn't use them much.
Justice was expensive,
so corners were fit
without, whenever the cost
was too great.

The son threw his hands in the air,
laughing and crying, "nail, nail"
when he heard the hammer do its work
as the nails were needed
by his Father.

# Father and Sons

Blue stripes.
Baby blue stripes.
And darker ones
In deep contrast.

He is a blue bird
Lighting briefly
On some twig
Overhead.
I can't reach him.

Born 13 weeks ago
And I was taken in.

Stripes on prison clothes
Worn long ago.
Clothes to warn others off
Blaring as foghorns:
These men are not safe,
Will never be safe again.
These men are prisoners.

He's not safe, I know it.
I can't, in the end, hold him
My time is temporary.

At 15 years, my son dresses only
In blue jeans and denim shirts
at least slightly dirty from work.

Another blue bird
Just older
Another prisoner.

I cannot help myself.
Denim and baby blue stripes
Aren't that different.
Stripes and denim draw me in. Contrast:
The prisoner,
The bluebird.

Neither knows his true name.
One too old, perhaps
Too experienced.
The other too young,
Lacking time and place.

Both flit
Twig from twig,
Making their own ways
Even now.

Such flitting drops a net over me.
I am imprisoned
And I am condemned
To love.

I shall never be but
their father
and they
my sons.

# Mother Made Life on Saturdays

When we were young,
my sister, brothers and I
would leave fairy tales and toys,
our hungry bodies buoyed
into the kitchen
on waves of sweetness
from the cookies, pies,
and biscuits Mom baked
on what seemed
like six days a week
—never Sunday,
for then we went to thank God
for the other six.
My favorite was Saturday,
for then Mom baked bread,
as she learned
from her mother.

We children could stand
at kitchen's edge
late on Saturday mornings,
after cartoons, and watch
the flour particles drift in
and out of the shafts of sunlight.
If we made too much noise, Mom would
shoo us out of the kitchen.
Then we could see the marks
tracing her hard work

as the flour clung to her blouse
where her belly met the counter
as she mixed her miracle—flour,
yeast, salt, sugar and oil
transformed into dough
from which we could never snatch
a piece.

She'd stir the dough
until it was stiff
enough to put onto the counter
awash in flour
where she'd knead it,
pounding, pushing, and pulling,
turning it over, like God did
with ancient clay until it
drew its first breath.
When Mom was done, how high
its chest rose
breathing in love.

She always set
a portion aside
for buns we'd have
after Saturday night supper.
Cooled down from the oven's heat
(we couldn't eat bread
right out of the oven!)
the butter still melted quickly.
Often she'd make chelsey buns
—cinnamon, butter, and brown sugar
rolled into sweetness itself.
At those suppers, we'd argue
over who had how many,
and who deserved the extra one,
if Mom had made thirteen,
instead of twelve.

The argument continued
at Sunday morning breakfast
as we'd push to get the end crust
a two-sided wonder
—crispy outside and
soft, moist, white inside.
Dad was no impartial judge
in these matters,
being no more patient
than we children.
The crust was always placed
on the bottom of the stack,
except when Dad cut the bread,
when the stack was turned upright,
and the crust landed on his plate.

My mother baked bread every Saturday
all through my young life,
into high school and college years.
There were times when
we were teenagers that
she baked bread twice a week,
for we'd eat two loaves
at Sunday breakfast alone.
And then there were our friends,
an assortment of relatives and
my father's teenage employees.

So she baked.
Was it just that she disliked
the flavorless texture
and the even slices
of what she called
store-bought, or rather that
her homemade bread extended

her life to ours and now my life
to her grandson as I've learned to bake
Saturday bread?

# Enchanted Rock

One spring day
while we were out
hiking Enchanted Rock,
while we were speaking of
reincarnation, my father's
consciousness slipped away
from the hospital where they had tried
to fix his heart. He floated somewhere
down by Front Street. Later
he ended up in St. Andrew's Cemetery,
looking over my granddad's grave.
In the fall when I went home
to take care of the estate,
his consciousness went home too,
as if he waited for me to say goodbye
to the enchanted rock of my childhood.

# Down on all Fours

Chasing
my young image
across the floor
he turns to see
whether I
am down on all fours
as if to ask
do you love me?

For a moment I am
Joseph chasing my young
God across the floor
when he turns to see
whether I
am down on all fours
as if to ask
do you love me?

# Communion of the Saints

I once saw Peter and Paul (and a host of others) sitting in church. I was surprised everyone could fit in the pews. (So many!—all heaven was there—yet no one was crowded. An ancient debate about how many angels could sit on the head of a pin was solved.) The saints were smiling (a few even laughing—in church no less!) when the children spoke their liturgy for growing up, a rite of passage, a palpable movement of the Spirit.

I was hoping Peter and Paul (at least) would stay for lunch afterward, in the undercroft, (a churchy word for basement, but I wanted to impress Peter and Paul!) while we patted our maturing youth on the back. They didn't. (Paul looked a little askance at me and stammered something about having eaten already).

Instead, Jesus came serving refreshments (French bread and Bordeaux, as I recall) and saying, "I made cake as well, to celebrate the children." When I asked why the others couldn't come to lunch, Jesus said "They've already eaten—besides, they are just frosting." Then he laughed and winked, ribbing me a bit with his elbow while he balanced a platter of olives and sliced tomato with his other arm. Then he babbled some words about heaven lacking the "merely decorative." He spoke like some aesthetician (not the type that works at Beryl's Beauty Bar but the philosophical type, one with a British accent). I felt like Peter and the other not-so-quick-witted followers probably did when Jesus used to trot out one of his old chestnuts: "The kingdom of heaven is like. . ..a ball of wax, a can of worms, a. . . . . ."

When I asked what he meant, Jesus gave me a quizzical look. "About what?"

"The frosting. . . . and the decorative," I replied, innocently enough, I thought.

"How long must I be with you?" he cried (a little sternly, it seemed to me.) "That's in Plato! That's in Plato! And you call yourself a teacher of...of....of the law and prophets!" Then he laughed again, this time throwing back his head and roaring!

When he caught his breath, he squeaked out: "You're almost as dense as that guy Nick who would only meet me at night. It was past my bedtime and I could still skate metaphorical circles around him." Then he was quiet while he served some antipasto to a friend of mine, Diotoma, an elderly woman, and her husband. (Her great grandmother was from the Greek islands someplace. The grandmother arrived here after the war. I liked Diotoma very much, but she hardly ever spoke).

I still wasn't sure what Jesus meant, and I was still stinging from his tone of voice. Since this was only the third time I'd seen Jesus up close, I thought I'd better clear something up. "I don't teach the law and the prophets. I teach philosophy!"

"I know that," said Jesus. "Remember, I saw Nathanael under the tree, and he believed on that very flimsy evidence." Slipping between two little kids, Jesus cast his eyes back to me but he was off, serving a third kid a cupcake and I was left alone.

I sat down beside Diotoma. She said nothing to me but looked tenderly at her husband and whispered (so I could hear) "I love you." Out loud, she said, as if to no one: "Goodness, truth, and beauty. They're all the same. Look under the skin, my child, look under the skin!"

I wondered what she meant.

# The Muse

*For Shirley Mullen*

The muse wouldn't come.
I waited and—!
No inspiration.
I was looking for the hook—
you know,
the first sentence.

Ha! Better be careful.
One can't demand
too much of the muse.
Maybe to ask for a sentence
is to ask for a

sentence. You know,
a long dry spell,
with no visitors.

# The Teacher

*For A. R. "Pete" Diamond*

Two days before it's over
he's drinking beer,
at Peabody's,
talking and laughing,
at revelations among us.

The student says he can't
understand the ontological
presence too hidden
even for clear description.

The teacher says the presence must be
here—we can't see how
but it is, else there's no reason
to laugh, be angry, or
drink beer

# The Teacher Again

*For A. R. "Pete" Diamond*

We wept again.
Tonight his time is passing
over to others
who will not
to live as he lives
telling jokes to make
our theories laugh out
into the dark:
Laugh lines on the face
of God.

# A commentary on the low flight of birds

*For Curt Peterson,*
*pastor, epiphany, and friend*

My soul is so heavy that thought can no more sustain it,
no wingbeat lift it up into the ether.
If it moves, it sweeps low to the ground
like the low flight of birds when a thunderstorm approaches.
Over my inmost being there broods a depression,
an anxiety that presages an earthquake.
              S.K.

This tutelage ravished him,
a man alone,
staggering up St. Peter's steps,
carrying *onus probandi*
(seeds of miscreance—*quantum sufficit*)
further than usual.

The impending baptism,
dark in its hour,
exposed hologrammatic stones
among the steps not real
enough to carry
the weight,
both man and burden.

One bird among the flock, a dove,
ravenous for truth, took the seeds one by one.
Together,

less heavy,
earthquakes no more precarious,
stones no more Achilles's heels,
the man
and the dove,
once again paced the steps.

# Creases and Furrows

> *In honor of Wendell Berry*
> *whose Royal standard typewriter*
> *makes for grace.*

God gave us gardens in which to plow
a furrow or two.
The lines were clear;
this way, not that, and yet. . .
and yet we didn't follow the natural
curve of the hill.

Instead we plowed as sane folk,
all whopper-jawed,
and moved the earth until its state
was marred beyond clear sight
of what it was and meant to be.

These furrows turned to creases,
dark ravines on the face of God.

# The Fundamentalist

Her house
just so,
her dress
unlinted,
her mouth
uncrumbed,
in case the Unseen Guest
showed up.

With one eye on
the dust she prays
to better
clean her house.
She's always
misread
that verse; it
swept her mind
the night the sawdust
covered the dirt.

She claims
this house
is not her home,
she's just
a-passin' through
the fun
she missed
denying life was worth
the dance,

again to
wash the floor
while others
moved with grace.

And when her life
is not unkind,
she still
denies
the orchestra
time, always keeping her
house uncluttered,
throwing the sheet music
into the fire

of hell,

of course:
as all
should know
to earn the keep
of God we must
be perfect
as He is,
perfect,
a clean house,
a clean heart.

No need for
grace at this address,
just hard work
and a clean cloth.

# Suits

He'd been to far too many to suit him.
His hands shook. Yet he walked
a half-a-dozen times or more almost
to the casket, his shoulders pulled up
like it was below freezing and his head
tilted slightly to one side.
He wanted to get close, but seemed to know
if he did, the body would leap up
in judgment.

Everyone had told her not to marry him.
All my life I'd heard it.
Marriage was for better or for worse, and
in her case, everyone said, it was for
Wes. But here they were, at her brother's funeral,
together after all those years of Labatt's beer.

I remember once he stopped drinking,
getting a job trimming branches
for the Water and Power.
I expected some words of praise for him,
but nothing. Then when
the daily drive past the Brewer's Retail
got the best of him, all I heard was
"poor Wes."

Was it Wes's imaginary judgment
from my grandfather's casket
he feared; perhaps that we'd laugh

at his less-than-formal clothes
holding together his wiry frame, bulging eyes,
unshaven face and all; that he'd
undeservedly outlived a better man; or
something else?

As I saw his eyes, they met mine,
in vague unrecognition.
But as always he greeted me
with a distinct but
Canadian "good day."
It was a greeting from my childhood,
one I used to get from a tougher school-mate,
a boy who almost died of some illness
I don't recall. I just remember
asking his parents about him each week
when I collected for the papers I delivered.
He lived and later made part of his living
selling drugs. He was always nice to me,
I guess because I asked about him.
Still, his "good day"
was a casket greeting.

As Wes lurched toward the casket for the
fourth or fifth time, my brother said,
"look at poor Wes."

But whence the poverty?
That we should be afraid
of death? Perhaps Wes
like my school-mate had
known its inside a long time.
Perhaps he had known too well the silky
feel of the casket and that some day
his funeral would finally
suit him.

# Rigor Mortis

Near freezing outside,
no water flooding the fountain,
granite benches lying about
unmoving, like so many
morticians's slabs.

No smoking allowed
inside the buildings so
there she sits,

taking a drag, a stiff
attachment to the granite,
her cigarette jammed between two thick,
unfeeling appendages
on a woolen-gloved hand.

# Long Time Down to Death

*In memory of Randy Harvie*

Long time down to death, a sentence pronounced, a slow train announced, a sacrament denounced. A small boy, just a kid too young to know your future. The omniscient doctors in Toronto revealed the news. It's a wasting disease, a failure to thrive, a deterioration. It's a long time down to death, hardly heard of 'til Jerry's kids made it the showplace of T.V., a household phrase: Muscular dystrophy. MD, for short, like your life. Muscular dystrophy. A fancy way to say you've entered the twilight zone, a slow, long time down to death, your muscles liquefying, including your heart. At ten, you look like a tall, skinny kid. By seventeen, you are so thin bean poles look like football players. Yet you keep on walking, your back curved into a question mark wanting to know "why?"

You told me once, whispered, really, as we talked ourselves to sleep in your stereo-wired room: "The left side of my back is getting awfully weak." A confession of friendship, two teenage boys, struggling to love one another, one knowing his death from the inside out, the other thinking he grew stronger every day. Brothers, hoping tomorrow will hold their futures together. It didn't. You told me once, not whispered, this time, "I'll never see those quacks in Toronto again. I don't want to be a guinea pig." You were tired of being poked and prodded like a skinny chicken wing at the corner meat shop, the residents ogling you, so much skin over bone. Later I discovered Piers Ploughman calling doctors butchers, killing thousands before their time. There wasn't much meat on your bones to butcher.

My best friend for a couple of years, you graduated ahead, worked for my dad, then yours, then set up a shop repairing radios and T.V.s—whatever came your way. You were an electronics genius. I admired you (was jealous?). Your singing voice, too. You sang at a Christmas concert before we were friends when we were kids. (Before that, you poked me with a pin at First Baptist's Mission Band. I cried, you laughed. I hated you, then, for that.) "I Wonder as I Wander" I hear it still, a crystal clear rendition, as good as any professional. I moved to California, got married, went to college, then seminary, then graduate school. You stayed home, married too. Norma. I hoped to be your best man, but we'd begun to wander apart. I wondered at your asking another friend, an older friend, to stand for you. It hurt but it was a wise choice on your part. I had begun to abandon the friendship.

You loved your dogs, grieving their deaths when your house burnt down, grieving them even while you rescued your niece from the flames, dragging her out behind your electric cart your arms too weak to pick her up. "Orillia Fire Department to Honor Disabled Hero." Funny, until that headline, I never thought of you as disabled. I just thought you would die young. You didn't see yourself as a hero, passing the honor back to the fire department, an irony lost on most, perhaps. You used to joke with your Dad, Al, that Orillia's fire department was great at saving basements. That they were heroes later showed how much you'd grown.

It's a surprise we didn't both die young. Once when we were in high school, I drove you to my house where my dad had you rewiring the electrical panel. (I was jealous then, too, for knowing what I didn't, for being selected for this technical job I couldn't have done, really). You leaned over, just as we rushed down the hill toward Bass Lake and turned off the ignition. It was an older GMC panel van, no autolock on the steering wheel, no power steering. I was surprised and angry yet managed to drive the truck to the bottom of the hill clutching and turning the six-banger engine back on. You laughed, and laughed, your head thrown back, your hands holding your knee up toward your chest, hardly catching your breath. Later that week, you were driving my parent's late-model Olds Cutlass S, a sporty red and white, very fast effort from Detroit: power steering, brakes, autolock on the wheel. I leaned over, turned it off (not, thank God, so it locked—I hadn't thought about that!). But the power-steering turned off with the engine. You were pissed, yelling at me, like I had betrayed you.

I was hurt, embarrassed, really. Years passed before I knew you were scared, and anger masked your fear, your arms not strong enough to steer without the power assist. It took me even longer to realize I, too, had been scared when you first turned off the key on the old GMC van, anger masking my fear.

You had lived more wildly than I, at least for Orillia. When I was 16 and you an older, more mature 17, you took me and my brother to the "Second"—the run-down version of the "First." Hotels both. We ordered beer and no one carded us—that was the Second, where no one carded and no one cared about our age. It was my first beer, at least in a bar. I remember wondering how you knew they would ignore the pimples on my face, my nervous and probably guilty look, and the truth that salt made cheap beer taste better.

We spent a week each over two summers at your family's cottage on Lake Naiscoot, north of Point au Baril, north of Parry Sound. We parked at the boat launch, went up-lake via boat for half an hour. Other than Toronto, Niagara Falls (with other school children) and one trip to Montreal for the 1967 Expo, (with my family) it was the furthest I'd ever been from home, less than 90 miles. But it wasn't the miles, it was the lake, a deep mystery, cold and haunting, that made it so far away. The first year, we "helped" your father build a sleeping cabin up the hill from the cottage, the deep, cold lake at the bottom of its steep sides. We were to carry the sheets of plywood up to the building site but we were too slow and your dad carried them by himself while we were off cavorting somewhere probably thinking about the German girls who lived down the lake and about whom we dreamed. Next year, we stayed in that cabin listening to Gordon Lightfoot as we drifted off to sleep. We talked about going to school together, renting an apartment. It never came to be. In some sense, you didn't need the education, genius you were with transistors, resistors and capacitors. I was meant for other things. I needed to get further away too, to find my roots and my adventure, going farther than Toronto,

Montreal, and Lake Naiscoot. Later, when your parents sold the cottage, I remember feeling deeply sad, a lifetime gone haunting in the mist.

We talked about God's power to heal, went to a Katherine Kuhlman convention. Our circle of friends prayed and prayed and prayed for your healing, but when the call came from Ms. Kuhlman you felt nothing and didn't go down for her prayers. She had said, "Come down if you feel God moving in you." You hadn't and didn't. I admired and defended you for listening to her, to God, and to yourself. Some of our other friends thought your faith was weak. I knew better. Later I'd learn even closer to hand: God doesn't heal everyone. The mystery was lost to us clouded in a mist like the ones that settled over Lake Naiscoot, lost to us like a dance among those who've joined the communion of the saints.

Were you happy, I wonder? You could tell a great joke, be funny off hand and off color. But you were depressed, too, as so many teenagers are. So was I. We were no different, once talking about me shooting you while you knifed me: serious but not really. Just talk among friends in pain. Then we laughed. Much later I visited you once in a while when I came home to Bass Lake. But that fell off like an apple from a tree. Was it ripe, or was it an early one, before its time? We moved on, me to teach college and you to your shop and later to your electric cart and then to your bed. When your father died, you were too weak to make the funeral. That, Norma said, was what finally moved you to your own funeral and a different sort of bed. I couldn't go, tied up in Oregon with my own issues. But I talked to Norma on the phone. She said that wherever you were, you were laughing and cavorting through fields filled with sunlight. There was some bitterness in Norma's voice; some sense, maybe, that faith had not done well by you or her. It might be true, but who am I to say?

We all thought, at 16, you'd live just a while. But you made your 50s. Remarkable, and maybe not such a long time down to death, a sentence pronounced, a slow train announced. What did those MDs in Toronto know? A life lived always involves a sacrament or two. While the disease took your muscles, I now know it didn't take your real heart, the one that steered the Olds, made you mad at the doctors and probably at God too. That heart gave you courage, and humor, and made you a good friend. Such hearts live in faith even when maybe the trappings drop off. You made me laugh and taught me about jealousy and anger and the first steps of friendship and intimacy with other men. I wish I'd stayed in touch, the one phone call a few weeks before you died wasn't enough. The apple fell before it was ripe.

Today, I'm missing you, nostalgic for our youth, nostalgic for your laugh, your knee pulled up to your chest with your head thrown back. You always made me smile. Cavort, my friend, cavort, wherever you are but this time, help your dad, with your big strong arms, to carry up those sheets of plywood and build that sleeping cabin on the other side of the cottage, up the steep hill beyond Lake Naiscoot.

# Episodes on the Eve of War: January 14, 1991

The wooden loon hangs crookedly
on the wall;
my aesthetics class went well.

About a year ago, while Germans chipped out the mortar
of 40 years of anger,
I told my freshman class
within a year
American would be at war.
I was wrong.

It was a year and two months.

One student says
if I can't get a job as a philosopher
maybe I can get a job as a prophet.

I tell her they kill prophets.

She says they kill philosophers.

She's right, of course
—no comfort there.

My wife says there's clothes to hang out.
The cat sleeps under the vent where the heater
warms up the room.

The sun's up in Saudi;
some grunt warms his breakfast
on the engine of his unit's tank.
The last supper maybe.

I hang the clothes—smell the baby's laundry smell,
and know that he might someday
be eighteen,
and drafted
and scared,
heating his

last supper on the grill
of a tank.

I think about the paper I've to write on religious pluralism. I can only think
of Islamaphobia, an instance of America's penchant to vilify whatever
is not American or
not on its side.

But that is too easy. It is my
penchant too. I've lost my roots,
in America. I think it's time to go to Canada—
home, but I know we're over there too.

The bed's not made
but it's time to sleep.
Five minutes til Nightline,
thirty five til the
fifteenth.

Our godchild called from Chicago tonight.
Her pastor's son—who's really smart and can quote the Bible to prove his

point—had her in fourteen-year-old
tears, feeling guilty for not being good, as the angel breaks the
second seal;
and here we are,
Armaggeddon tomorrow.

Damn evangelicals, dispensing prophecies like so many
easy-to-read fortune cookies:
Gorbachev another anti-Christ,
war tomorrow,
famine next week.

# Messiah

> "the woman which hath an husband that believeth not,
> if he be pleased to dwell with her, let her not leave him."
>
> I Corinthians 6:13

### I

The bread was white. He turned
it over and over. His coarse fingers,
calloused hard by years
of working the fields,
found the bread strange.

Her flesh was white. He turned
her over, and his gentle hands,
worn smooth by years
of caressing her warmth,
found her body strange.

Fifty-odd years of eating
the body of Christ. Fifty-odd
years of loving his wife. Gone.
He crushed the bread.

### II

It was a wonder he ate the bread at all,.
He thought it all a myth, but not just any
myth; one that kept her
happy. That's why he went

all these years. That's why,
after he milked the cows and fed the chickens,
once a week he walked
into the house to bathe and don his
Sundays. That's why
he ate the bread and drank the cup.
A happy home was worth a few baths
and some unnecessary meals.

### III

Now she was gone; no need for Sundays
anymore. He still had to milk the cows, of course,
and feed the chickens. That was work. But no more
myth chasing; no more free
wine and mirth for him. Still
that he had crushed the bread that last Sunday
kept him awake, sometimes
he could almost hear
a cry.

### IV

He could not live long alone.
He went to visit a few church friends.
They welcomed him.
After a while he showed up
a Sunday or two,
here and there.
But no bread for him;
not the myth.

### V

He still called out to her,
months after she was gone.

Inside each other's skins,
breathing the same air and
drinking the same water
for fifty-odd years,
he couldn't leave her;
one flesh,
she never left
his unbelief.

   VI

One Sunday, absent-mindedly, he took
the bread off the silver tray.
By then it was too late.
He couldn't bring himself
to throw it away.
He heard the voice "come not
because you must but
because you may."

He understood what she said.
The feast was his.
No longer would he be alone.
He was finally pleased
to dwell with her.

# Unless a seed dies

*For Ian*

Here stand I, not quite alone,
a withered grey oak, not able any more
to push down roots nor skyward send my
green pleas for aid.

                      The younger trees have grown,
crowding out the space needed
for older ones like me, all
spindly and bare. And yet
though dead
I live.

This morning a sparrow landed on my branch,
and pecked a bug from between my
wizened teeth. The sparrows live
as do the bugs who slowly cycle my
old bones to soft shale, slagging off my inner
parts to change; to bring new life where once
I stood, the world remade by mystery
ever changing.

                      So sing I, the old and grey,
no bark, nor leaves, nor swaying
windward. I break, I fall
into the ground,
one last time,
to see, to hear,
to know,

the way of God
in resurrection.

# As much about me as Joey

Joey lived down the road during the summers in a tall A-frame cottage across the road from the right-of-way access to the lake. The cottage stood astride the surveyor's lines, one leg of the A on somebody else's property. The error wasn't discovered until years later, after the property had changed hands several times. The owners didn't know about it, apparently. Later, when the real estate sign hung gathering moss, my dad said the place would be nothing but headaches for a buyer. To skid the A-frame across the property line would be no small job.

Joey's dad was a mustached, potbellied man who worked for the township. Occasionally I'd see him in the winter clearing the local roads with a snow plow but more often on hot summer Saturdays standing in the yard in his undershirt, smoking a cigarette. Joey's mother was shorter and thinner; pretty and nice to us neighbor kids. I remember her making Freshie for us on steamy afternoons.

Joey was olive-skinned, active in the Sea Scouts, and owner of a Daisy BB gun just like the one I coveted every year when the Simpson-Sears Christmas catalogue came in the mail. Hunting seemed a big deal for Joey's family. My dad had no guns and no desire to hunt. All the neighbor boys played "guns." It was our favorite game in the fall and the spring—when the cottagers deserted us for the comfort of town or city life and when the snow had not made war strategy too difficult. Only then did we have the run of all the yards with nothing to bother us, neither people nor weather. Since my family lived on the lake where the cottagers came and went with the leaves, the gang of boys would meet at our house to plan battle strategies. During the early fall, my dad used to pull the wooden dock out of the lake and lean up its two pieces against the house at a certain spot. They kept most of the snow out of the pit dug to allow for a door to my family's recently constructed, and unfinished, basement. The dock ran the water away from the basement when the snow melted in the spring. When the war games were on, all of us boys would sit on the partially dismembered dock and choose two captains from among the older boys. They, in turn, would pick members for their sides. We'd then lay out the boundaries—south to the edge of Nelson's yard and north to the other side of the right-of-way, but not beyond MacDonald's, east to the far side of the cottage no one ever seemed to use, and west to the lake shore. This included the A-frame property. Then we'd stalk each other, fighting over our imaginary lands. Most of the fights were about which of us shot which first. The bigger boys usually won these skirmishes by sheer brawn.

In the heat of the battle once, my stick gun in hand, I remember meeting my dad as he cornered our house. He mumbled something about how terrible war was. I didn't understand what we were enacting, not completely. The Vietnam war was in full swing, but we were Canadians, and none of our brothers was off in the jungle. Still we played at war and other games. We felt free to run in all the cottage yards. A variety of tags, hide and seek, and red rover, red rover filled the hours. So we roamed. Or played with what the summer's children had carelessly left behind. I had a fort in the space where the old, above-ground gas tank once stood in our yard, its hand pump jutting into our lane. There I had stashed a blue and white plastic toy boat some renter's child had left in his yard by the beach.

Theft wasn't the only crime we committed. One spring two or three of us boys caught a frog, put it in an old rag, and rolled it mercilessly through the hand-cranked rollers used to wring out Joey's family's swimming suits. The rollers were mounted with large bolts, I suppose, to a tree behind the A-frame. I doubt I committed the act itself; I was too chicken. But I remember the cranking of the handle. I remember seeing the frog's life crushed out of the rag and onto the rollers. I think I ran away then, but I'm not sure. I know I never killed another frog just for the thrill. I remember the next summer seeing the death-stain of the frog on the rollers. I kept the secret to myself. That was, I think, one of the last times Joey's family came for the summer.

Their A-frame was empty during the seasons of war, just like all the other cottages. Still, Joey wasn't far away, since his family didn't live in town. Their permanent home was only a few miles distant, two or three township roads to the east. And we boys fought over the A-frame property, so Joey was never far away mentally. But he came bodily onto the scene during June, July, and August. All the neighbor kids played together during the long summer days, the sun setting long after nine. To cool the white-heated afternoons, we'd go swimming in the lake. Usually I had to swim in front of our house—we lived there all year round so it couldn't be called a cottage. The diving raft at the right-of-way was public, though, and its allures, along with the much sandier beach, called daily. When one of the mothers or older sisters was unburdened from her household chores and free to watch us, I could sometimes avoid our rocky bottom and jump repeatedly from the raft down the road, across from the A-frame.

One summer Joey wanted to build a tree fort. It was after I'd tired of the fort on the ground. We tried a big elm beside the apple trees in our lane. We got as far as the fort's floor. We had to build it with the joists in the shape of an A, since there was nowhere to nail a forth corner. I remember Joey tried to convince the rest of us to make the fort square by suspending the unbuilt corner in mid-air. The A-shape won, but we never finished the fort. It was open to the sky, with no roof or walls. And it never had a ladder leading up to the sloping floor. We always had to climb the tree to get to the fort, and there was always the threat that the slope would get to be too much for us. Later, Joey's father built another tree fort. It was square and solid, built between three trees behind the A-frame cottage. Two trees formed the legs for one side, a third for the other. The third tree stood equi-distant from the other two and one floor joist could be balanced, an equal length jutting out on either side of the tree, to form a fourth side. It had a roof. It hid no stolen toy boats. Joey and a bunch of us boys were playing in the fort once when I decided to shimmy down the third leg of the fort. I was wearing shorts, which I detested as sissy. I caught the flesh of my right leg, close up to my crotch, on a nail that, apparently, Joey's father had left protruding from the tree. I still have the scar. My mother patched me up, but there were lots of jokes among my father's teen-age employees about what I narrowly escaped losing.

We went back and forth between the two forts, but often preferred the one we boys had built. I always liked its shape, despite Joey's protests.

During the summers Joey taught me. He was a year older and vastly more world wise. His father had beer in the fridge. My father didn't drink but for once or twice a year. Joey taught me how to make cigarettes out of dried corn silk. No one in my family smoked. Joey had a foul mouth; we all had foul mouths, like the boys in 1980s movies. We didn't talk that way around our parents. Nor did we know what the words meant, except Joey. A sort of summer tutor, he talked about the "eagle's nest"—the top floor of the A-frame, reachable only by ladder, where his father and mother slept together, alone, on hot, sticky nights; the sweaty, mustached, potbellied man and his sweet-smelling, thinner, pretty wife.

Joey's family usually didn't go to church, or at least not like my family did. My family didn't use "God" or "Christ" as expletives. "Damn" was okay for my parents. "F***" was out. Even I knew that. When another family moved into the area from the city and the kids used "God" and "Christ" freely in front of their parents, I, too, felt free to do so—in front of their parents. I used to walk to school with them. Their mom typically walked with us, since she felt her youngest boy too little to go without her. Once I, appealing to a profound, new sense of liberation with this adult, said "F***." We were half-way up the hill, right in front the White's house. She was walking at my left side. Just a second after I uttered the fateful word, I glanced over my shoulder and slightly to my back. As well as I remember our location and my action, I better recall her expression. Her face grew flushed, her eyes fairly danced, and the muscles in her neck grew taut. It was clear she disapproved. I was so unaware, I didn't know what I'd done to merit her anger until years later. The word had no referent beyond my curse; I didn't know what it meant.

Joey did. He talked about f***ing, in whispered tones around the other boys. He once told me that f***ing occurred when two men rubbed their penises together. I didn't believe it. I knew it had something to do with Joey's parent's need of an eagle's nest. I knew boys were different from girls; I'd even seen the difference up close. Boys weren't the only kids in the neighborhood. But girls didn't talk with boys about f***ing, although sometimes they would explore their bodies with the boys. There were lots of empty cottages around during the school year, and not everyone locked the doors. The ones that stood locked against our exploration were mysterious, but I didn't force entry. Joey's cottage was one of the open back doors, sometimes, but the front door was always locked. Although we could have, we didn't spend much time inside the unlocked cottages. When we did, it was only to explore. We knew it was at least risky. Once my older brother got caught in a neighbor's cabin. He was strapped to the point where my mother remembers it still; it stands out among the punishments.

Because Joey didn't live far from us during the school year, we saw each other regularly. In fact, we attended the same school. But we hardly ever spoke to one another. He was a whole grade ahead of me and that chasm was too large to bridge. It was as if he lived in a foreign country with which my country was barely holding diplomatic relations. So we didn't play much together other than during summers. We both had other friends. I don't recall his, but mine were Steve, John, Ray, and Rick. Other than Rick, who lived just up the road, I hardly saw these boys during the summers.

Joey took his life when we were in our twenties. I do not know why. We had lost touch. I had long since left home to go to school and work. Joey had not. I lived in California. Joey lived in our hometown. My mother calmly stated, in the middle of a letter about her garden and Dad's busy work schedule, that Joey had killed himself. Did I remember him?

How could I not? Two different worlds. Joey is long since gone, and I have a mustache and a potbelly now. I don't own a gun.

I'd love to own an A-frame summer cottage. I want it to be on a lake with a sandy beach. And it needs to be right on the beach, not simply across from a right-of-way.

# The Third Day

Two weeks ago Tuesday, a friend drowned.
Forty-seven. No more hope I guess.
Headlong, he went into the lake
just out from the beach where we used
to swim each summer afternoon.
His canoe was found upside down.

The peace ruptured. Everyone
was out in boats, my mother said.
Seeking. Gaping. Rummaging.
Clues to my friend's mortality.

Mother worried, thinking he'd surface nearby,
buoyant up along the shore, doing the
dead-man's float, like we did when we were
children. Except he'd be doing it more
effectively.

She sat long ago waiting.
We played and splashed,
forded boats in the water and floated,
holding our breath, face-side down.

Children rarely swim there anymore.
Zebra muscles have taken all the beaches.
An alien submarine navy, skulking on the
bottom of some civilian's boat, they attacked
one summer day after my childhood.

Foreign to the waters,
off-landers from another habitat.
Sharp as razors, they cut children's feet,
and clog up water-supply lines,
a plaque choking the arteries of life.

The ducks remain the same,
not an immigrant among them.
Mallards swim near the bank, and once in a while
a loon floats like a ghost on a foggy morning,
singing solitary songs, picking off the occasional,
if unfortunate, fish.

Death isn't new to the lake,
but my friend's body was a foreign object,
unsettling the minds of the neighbors.

My mother was anxious she'd spy my friend first,
afraid he'd come by for an untimely visit.
My dad's teenage employees of thirty years before
made unseasonable social calls.

They mostly drove delivery trucks and
surprised her when they dropped by the house
at all hours of the day, and sometimes night.

Like her own children, they needed something:
To eat, to talk, to tell about their new loves.
My mother cared and listened and cajoled.

They came to get a hug or a pat on the back.
Sometimes they needed a good swift kick,
as she would say, on the seat of the pants.

She wrote me, the day after my friend drowned.
"The canoe floated out, in front somewhere,
upside down . They are still looking for him."

She sat and waited again, and wrote as if he were
 a little kid who'd gone to the store, gotten lost,
and now the neighbors were searching for him,
knowing he'd just gone over to a friend's house.

She knew he hadn't. She knew, instead, the shore.
She knew the lake would bare my friend's soul,
in ways she couldn't bear the burden of.
No possibility of a hug, or a pat,
or even a gentle kick on the seat of the pants.

Later she wrote again: "Still no sign of them
finding the body. I just hope he doesn't come
up in front of my place. They say they rise
on the third day, so it makes one wonder."

It had been four days when she wrote this
post-prophetic word. They found him
later that day, tucked among some weeds,
almost like he was playing hide and seek.
Or planting new seedlings among the
sugar maples he loved.

"They say they rise on the third day."
Some sort of biblical prophecy?
 A bit of old testament wisdom?
A truth cast on the waters, by the hand of God,
for scuba divers and dredge operators?

Perhaps a bit of folklore she got
from my ever-wise grandfather?
I remember him and my dad talking.
Someone floated up, in Lake Couchiching,
years ago. Maybe in the old times
rising up on the third day

was the only means of finding people lost
to the lake. Or maybe my grandfather
who used to help with men being baptized by
his church, had some special insight.

A year ago my friend went into a different body of
water. He was baptized by a local minister.
Maybe my mother was right and as they say,
"they rise on the third day."

But I think my friend may only
know a different kind of rising,
with a different kind of body ,
and a different kind of water.

I hope he's finally been
found and that he did rise,
on the third day.

# Take a Little Water

The ancient philosopher Thales suggested that everything is made of water. Of course, we know better. We say that everything is made up of very tiny particles swirling about other particles for no particularly obvious reason. But think about it. Why would Thales have held to the view that everything is made of water? Well, whenever you cut open some living thing, what comes out? Water. And when we wake up in the morning, what's on the ground? Water. And what falls from the heavens above? Water. And when we dig into the ground, what do we find? Water. We know that nothing can live without water. Water is everywhere and is central to living things.

In the tradition of the Church, there are two central sacraments, baptism and communion. The first, of course, has water as its central sign, while communion has wine and bread. Now neither wine nor bread would be what they are without water. In fact, when C.S. Lewis talks about Jesus' miracle of turning water into wine, he notes that more or less all that happened was Jesus speeding up the conversion of water (which is the major component of grape juice) into wine. Even unleavened bread has water in it.

So water is connected to nearly everything important to us, not only as people but as Christians. Even the two fundamental sacraments of the Church are linked via water. Baptism introduces us to the Church and frees us to participate in the body and blood of Christ.

Now picture yourself sitting on the banks of the Jordan. You're a Jewish peasant farmer whose come out to hear the prophet speak, to see the man dressed in a camel's hair cloak proclaim the kingdom of heaven. Let's suppose John the Baptist has been preaching. He's larger than life as he stands on the bank of the river, calling down the fire of heaven onto the sins of Israel. He is urging all the children of Israel to humble themselves before God, to seek God's forgiveness, and to be baptized for the forgiveness of their sins. People are lining up now to be baptized, to wash away their sins in their repentance. Some of the local religious leaders come up and seek also to be baptized. John calls them a brood of vipers. He tells them they must show their repentance by changed lives. He warns them that they cannot hide behind the fact that they are Abraham's children, for if God wanted, he could raise up Abraham's children from the stones! John continues by proclaiming the coming Messiah, the Holy One of Israel, the one who will baptize not just with water by with fire and the Holy Spirit, the one of whom John is not worthy to untie the sandal.

Then it happens. A man walks up. You are sitting close enough to hear this conversation. John says that he won't baptize him, but that the man should be baptizing John. But the man says, "let's do this so righteousness can be fulfilled." John agrees and so baptizes the man. As the man comes up out of the water, the heavens open up and he sees the Holy Spirit descending upon himself like a dove. A voice from heaven is heard. It says, "This is my Son, the Beloved, with whom I am well pleased."

People are shocked. This man John baptized is the greater prophet, the one to whom John points, the one who will baptize not just with water but with fire and the Holy Spirit! He's the one. Here you are, sitting, watching, wondering whether you should be baptized by John or not. Now you know. You need to follow this new prophet, the one blessed not just by John the Baptist but by God himself. This is the very Son of God! So you follow this new prophet, this one at whose baptism you heard the voice of the Lord God announcing, "this is my Son, the Beloved, with whom I am well pleased."

Come back now to the present, to reflect upon what this baptism means. Jesus tells John that the baptism will "fulfill all righteousness." Of course, we know that Jesus is without sin of any kind. What does it mean, then, for him to be baptized with John's baptism? To fulfill all righteousness: what does that mean? There are two people involved in this baptism, John and Jesus. John at first tries to prevent Jesus from receiving John's baptism. His reason is simple: I need to be baptized by you, and yet you come to me for baptism? But Jesus says, "Let it be so now; for it is proper for us in this way to fulfill all righteousness." There is a shift from John's concern for himself in his unworthiness to Jesus' emphasis on "us." I think part of the point in this text is simply the community nature of baptism. Baptism is not merely for the forgiveness of sins, but it is to introduce us into the community that is the church.

What is really important is that Jesus here identifies himself with us. It is his humble submission to John's baptism that signifies Jesus' true humanity, his true oneness with us. John has already told us that he is not worthy to untie Jesus' sandals. He tells Jesus that he should be baptized by Jesus, not the other way around. But Jesus—together with John—agree to baptism "that all righteous be fulfilled."

What is the key here? Jesus humbles himself and thereby receives the Holy Spirit. He recognizes himself as fully human, as one with a will that he could flaunt. Instead, he wills himself to the Father, and the Father, in return, tells everyone who can hear, "this is my Son, the Beloved, with whom I am well pleased."

Jesus and John fulfill all righteous in the simple act of Jesus humbling himself, aligning his will with the will of the Father. What humanity was meant to be, Jesus is. Righteousness is made manifest in Jesus' willing amalgamation of his will to the Father's will. His baptism is a death to himself and an aliveness to God. So is ours. We Christians all pass through the waters of baptism. We all die to ourselves and become alive to God. In baptism the Holy Spirit brings us into the Church and seals us with the love of God. Yet we daily have to reaffirm our baptismal vows. Daily we have to turn from Satan, to turn, indeed, from our own desires and ways, and turn toward God for guidance, sustenance, strength, wisdom, peace, happiness.

With Jesus' baptism, we have the beginning of his ministry. So with our baptism. We recognize our humility, our need for the Lord. We also recognize the role of the community. That is why we bring our children to the baptismal font. We are the community called the Church and we bring our children to the Lord for inclusion in that community, promising to live our lives before the children in such a way that the children will grow to know the Lord. Something happens in baptism. We are marked as God's. As we grow in the Lord, our baptismal vows are never far away. They are words spoken that reflect our lives. Jesus shows us the way with his own baptism. He shows us his humanity, his connectedness to us. He shows us that in our baptism, we are empowered by the Holy Spirit to live our lives as "fulfilling all righteousness."

We see water all around us. As Thales noted so long ago, everything is made of water. While not literally true, there is a powerful lesson in this ancient philosopher's tale. The Holy Spirit who alighted on Jesus "like a dove" is the same Holy Spirit who moved on the waters covering the earth and created the world. This is the same Holy Spirit who lives in us as Christians, empowering us to love and serve, hope and trust, live and share.

The dove here is not unimportant. Think of the dove sent out by Noah. That dove too flew around over the waters covering the earth, looking for life. When the olive sprig was found, the dove returned to Noah, new life growing out of death. So in our baptism. What Jesus had by nature, we can have by grace: the power to make our wills united to the loving will of the Father. This is the journey we are on. This is the path we trod. It is a path through the waters of baptism, through the waters of death, to the glorious kingdom on the other side.

And yet. . . . we must read on. Right after the baptism of Jesus, the Spirit of God takes Jesus into the wilderness to be tempted by the devil. For our part, we walk the path that leads through baptism. Along that path we feel the call of the devil. We feel the call of the old self wanting to go its own way. That is why the baptismal vows cannot be forgotten. That is why those words must be reaffirmed daily. We must renounce Satan and all the spiritual forces of wickedness. We must renounce the evil powers of this world. We must renounce all sinful desires that draw us from the love of God. We must turn to Jesus and accept him—again—as our Savior. We must put our trust in his grace and power. We must promise to follow and obey him as our Lord. Then the challenge in the wilderness will be overcome. And we shall be transformed. The likeness of Jesus will become our likeness. All righteousness will be fulfilled.

Our baptism is the baptism of Jesus, by fire and by the Holy Spirit. Let us not think of our baptism as some distantly past event, but think of it as current and living in us, giving us power, strength, wisdom and courage. Let us prepare ourselves to face down the Evil One in whatever guise he may show up. He prowls around, like a roaring lion, seeking someone to devour. Let us hear his roar and cover ourselves with the Holy Spirit through whom victory is given to us. Let us remember that Jesus is our brother. He humbles himself and receives John's baptism, "for it is proper for us in this way to fulfill all righteousness." He is in the community and baptism is a community thing. Jesus is a human just like us but who always follows the Father's will. All righteousness is fulfilled in him. But we, too, can share in that righteousness, for he is one of us, baptized and open, therefore, to following the Father.

So, take a little water.

# Euhemerists

On heads of pins
mortals dance,
changed to gods.

categories and intuitions,
foundation to a world.

immortal life,
freewill and God;
three unstructured
fragments,
failing design

outside the lore we move,
smug in our work,
the euhemerists,
changing myths to gods:
philosophers dancing.

# The Philosopher's Hill

The old philosopher, bent with aged questions,
grubs his way slowly up the hill.
He's alone now, lost in thoughts,
all lively ideas long since gone.
Seeking the cogito among his dreams,
he's left outside the circle where
he might have found the story.

The old philosopher, bent with aged questions,
once heard the call, but demanded too much.
I thought he misheard the muse thinking
the carol sung by a siren. Perceiving
rugged rocks he sailed about,
seeking assurance, a place to hide.
Yet if the truth be known.

The old philosopher, bent with aged questions,
once heard the call, but demanded too much.
He wanted to be a god, knowing.
An old and powerful mistake, really.
As old and powerful as the garden itself.
Weakness of the will, philosophers say.
Euphemism deeply rooted.

The old philosopher bent the aged questions
to his own taste. bound by hubris,
he wanted solidity first, not second.
Left alone, to his own devices,
the old man grubs his way

slowly up the hill,
Olympus.

# Advent Meditation on Ecclesiastes

Wisdom dwells among us, yearning
its fancies, fathoming, the hopeless task,
setting eternity in human hearts,
moving first to last.

Wisdom dwells among us, living
they hope, knowing they die,
eating the bread,
drinking the wine.

Wisdom dwells among us, writing
the endless, charming the words: warning!
well-driven nails, one shepherd;
advent of the
truthmonger.

# Time

Uncreated darkness,
empty, naught.

It was evening,
it was morning,
light spilled over
the edge,
splashing here,
there, washing
naught into
goodness.

No clocks ticked,
but sun and
moon and
stars danced without
effort, and time
began.

A simple picnic
in a garden,
an apple, and time
fell, bouncing off the
sun and
moon, and planets
coursing through
naught. Time lost its
focus.

So nightly we read our prayer,
*phos hilaron*, watching darkness
descend.

Each morning we ask,
the sun arrives,
spills over the edge, and
time is sanctified
again.

# The Farm Photograph

I saw today an old farm.
The house, barn, and chicken
coop stood erect on the graves
of fifteen generations of farmers.

Another outbuilding stood
to the south, across the road
which led to the markets,
whose mouths were always open.
The road divided the farm, as if the county
surveyors were against it. The farm
had grown up ignoring the officials
whose food production policies
always tried to divide the farm
against itself. They also
were hungry.

The farmers crossed the road
in rebellion:
on foot, by horse,
on wagon, by tractor;
on sheer strength of will,
on knowing the land,
by love,
by character.

The road was tree-lined,
the fields snow-covered,
in their orderly, angular cuts
into the ancient glacier's art.

The photo too was angular,
taken from a plane, high above
the smell of the feed lot;
away from the land,
away from bent backs,
away from hands that
loved it.

The feed lot was patterned
light gray to dark,
the closer to the barn,
the darker. But the light
of the sun cast long shadows
to the late December freeze.
Beyond the barn and dwelling,
the house-filtered light
undressed
to a church
with a steeple.

The fields were stark in contrast—
white as crisp sheets, a cover
for my farmer grandfather as he lay
dying. The fields went on forever—
off the glossy page. The road headed east,
increasingly shaded by trees until
it disappeared,
under cover.

# Pioneer Settlement in Muskoka:
# An Agri/Cultural History

*Ag History*'s essay promised
an explanation why
the farming failed,
a promised unfulfilled.

The southern body of Canadian shield
ran its fingers just into Orillia township
and onto the back of my forebear.

It was its hand that bent his body
to claw and scrape and tear
those bony appendages loose
their geologic grip
on acidic soils,
always liberating
next year's promising harvest.

Jim Phillips owned a rock farm,
a few wealthier neighbors said.
The essay agreed.
      Nothing
grew on it, save some strong
legs and arms—bone,
muscle, tendon—and layers of
blisters turned callous to
rock and ridicule.
Soil too thin,
heart and skin too thick.

The essay tells it
false.
    The pioneers didn't make mistakes
built simply on blind ignorances.
        They made
homes and friends and families, reaching out
over the shield even now.
      Hope
is the blind side of ignorance,
my great grandfather's
stubbornness gone just slightly atilt the reach
of all the experts in Ottawa.

He died on his rock farm, a family
planted, nurtured, and grown.

# In Anselm's Cave

*In memory of St. John,
on reading Anselm's prayers.*

I sit in the dark, flickers of light
stark against the uneven wall.
For once, the cave is still.
Tonight no one wills to walk.
The floor by the fire is vacant.
Phantom-casting images,
manikins, and false persona
staved off. My soul is quiet.

I am a vassal to my blindness,
my deafness, my chains;
to images I sense aren't true.
I wait, silent. A noise so small
I would have missed it in my breath.
A creak of leather against leather,
a sandal worn nearly out on the beaches
of Patmos.

Who goes there? I cry, breathing
curses against the torch.
Could it be the beloved one whose
scorching light overwhelms the fire,
whose adopted mother is herself nearly
divine, come to unfasten my chains?

I've wondered at this light in my dreams,

caught up to heaven. What grace is this?
Saved since birth, yet lost in grievous sin,
I scratch and claw this too steep climb toward
a light more whole, to pain my eyes
and cauterize my soul.

Arduous the way, the beloved walks along.
Love two-pronged alights the torch.
He is for me, for all the saints.
He leaned his head upon a breast
so fair, and love indwelled. We saints
pray and ask for aid, for truth revealed,
for love unveiled.

Salvation comes once more, the cave recedes,
but not so far. I fear to trip and fall again, new
fetters to make fast, an even blanker bulwark
than ever I've watched before. Save me John,
pray to our Lord from whom all good things come.
Leave me not alone but welcome me
among the saints, the friends who sentry
heaven's rampart, perfecting prayers for
those below who lie about in stupors
yet unknown.

# Scything with Friends

Oregon's summer sun peeks over the ridge.
Early morning and I stand watching a slow
roast of yesterday's mowed grass.

I bought a scythe. Crazy. Philosopher. Priest.
Not a farmer. A friend laughs. Neighbors say
'look, crazy philosopher, scything.' True.

A parishioner saw monk's robes
flowing along with grass.
Humorous. Medieval joke.

No sleek body mine, swaying in the field, as if
struck by the Holy Spirit. I laughed.
A Mad Farmer goes before me, against the grain.

Rowan forms waves. Savory grass a golden tide,
washing my field. God's wonder in grass filling my
nostrils, God's work with me. Mowing every day.

Pretty much forty minutes or so. Each morning.
Seemed enough to get the job done. Only half
the field's cut. New grass filling in sooner

than I can move. Will I ever finish? The swishing,
swishing of that blade. The swinging, swinging of my
body. A call. Out I go. Morning after morning.

Huge ant mounds, nearly a foot tall. Live bee nests.

Two so far. Bumble bees don't move any faster than I do,
thank God. Uneven ground. The swish, swish of the scythe.

Pleasanter than a power mower.
Look back. See what my hands have wrought.
Amazing windrows fall into place as straight as I can move.

Old memories float behind me: My granddad worked so hard.
He smiled that day I helped bring in the hay.
Home from college. In my twenties. Ignorant of grass.

He was retired then for six, maybe seven years.
He looked to be in trance.
Leaned on his ancient fork.

A break from pitching up.
I looked a fool, embarrassed at not knowing
how to use a fork.

The Mad Farmer was right. Pushing on pull doors.
Moving against the grain. Not the only way of living.
One way.

Something to be said: For scything.
For being a mad priest, a mad philosopher.
For having mad farmers as friends.

# Mortar and Pestle

*For Joann Harrison*
*Christmas, 2002*

An ancient Sarah
leaned over
cedar shavings
striking stones
one against another,
like a man and a woman
together too long,
sparking fire
where no fire was
before.

Arthritic hands
crushed wheat to meal,
pestle dropping,
mortar thudding,
baking bread
again for strangers
Abraham dragged home
excitedly whispering
something about
gods. Gods he liked, yet
fire kept him distant,
unless some voice told him
otherwise. The voice sent him
out here, to the middle of
nowhere. There was no fire,
except Sarah made it.

Bread she made
for Abraham and
all three—all strangers,
really, even
Abraham.
She heard them,
faces without smiles.
She snickered,
hiding her face,
the folds of the tent
covering her wrinkles,
hoping the strangers
wouldn't hear.
Or she laughed
out loud,
roared, even, at the
absurdity of men,
thinking they could
pick a winner in the
next race, or see through
the summer about
next fall's crop,
or hear the cry
of a woman in
childbirth.

She wasn't wrong,
this woman of old age,
who doubted the miracle
announced like so much
porridge set on the table.
She'd heard men before,
talking in whispered tones
women weren't to hear,
and now she was out
nowhere,

baking bread
for strangers.
She learned mistrust
from living with
such strangers, men who
know.

She was still attracted
to Abraham. He was old,
yes, but sinewy,
his skin tanned deep brown
from working the fields and his hands
hard from clipping the sheep.
But he had good qualities,
and his sinews still went all the way
down. Even at his age,
everything still
worked. Yet pleasure was
all she got,
and that not all
the time.
And she got no child. She
waited
and waited but
years passed,
her womb a stone.
She even gave in to Abraham after
she watched his eyes wandering
over the supple body of the
young Hagar.
He, too, was doubting the
strangers, and besides,
his sinews still went all the way
down.

Sarah wondered if
her womb was dead.
That's what everyone
said, that children didn't
come from women who
sinned, or from women
against whom
Yahweh had some
cosmic grudge.
But deeper down, she
wondered
if Abraham's sinewy
nature choked off
the seed. This was a thought
she dared not offer.
But still she wondered—until
Hagar conceived and
brought forth the father of
another nation.

So Sarah waited,
believing somehow she was
to blame. What were those strangers
talking about, that her old,
cold womb would
somehow make a
child, let alone a
nation? She awaited
the striking of the pestle
against the mortar,
of his flint against her
stone. She felt her womb
everyday, shrinking.
But she waited and
prayed. The laughter
amidst the folds

of the tent turned
to pleas for Yahweh
to open the folds, and let out
the child she stored inside,
the laughter turned to pleas
for the pestle to strike a fire in her long
quiet womb. At ninety,
who can wish
a monthly cycle?

Abraham, too, wondered, yet
daily he hoped,
hope turned to faith
as often as he could
muster. He entered her
tent, and waited. The rest
is lost in history,
the free acts of creatures
turning.

There was no sin, no
cosmic grudge, just
the hand of God,
moving over an
ancient womb,
God writing the story
through people making
their own choices.
Sarah conceived,
Isaac was born,
and the laughter of
disbelief turned to the
laughter of dance
at this miracle. Sarah
loved Isaac, and
the strangers didn't come
again.

Abraham rejoiced this son,
and Sarah protected Isaac,
nurtured him amidst the threat,
perceived or otherwise,
of serpents and wild beasts,
of poison plants and rushing waters,
of Hagar and Ishmael.
Abraham, in fear,
perhaps in anger,
cast Ishmael out,
his mother as well,
to fend for themselves.

They did, and they
do. Where was Abraham's voice
then? Where was his
knowledge of tomorrow
on the day
Hagar packed,
taking Ishmael
by the hand,
alone?

Sarah never dreamed Abraham
a threat.
Then came the voice,
the voice which said,
"Take this son,
your son,
the son you love,
your only son,
to Mount Moriah, and there,
sacrifice him to
me."

Sarah cried and pleaded.
Off went Abraham, a slave, a donkey
some wood, no lamb and
Isaac. Sarah wept.
She'd have been better off with
Hagar and Ishmael,
some serpents, beasts,
poison plants
and rushing waters.
Abraham seemed
a fool.

Sarah waited,
watched the figures shrink
small in the distance
powerless to stop them.
When she could see them no more
she went to her tent,
dropped on her face,
and cried out. "God,
oh God, why take
this son, my son,
the son I love,
my only son? I'll take
no meat nor bread,
no water nor wine,
until they return."
She prayed and pleaded,
negotiating reality with Yahweh again.
"Please, please make this fool
stop." God heard her voice,
reneged, and caught the ram
in the thicket
on Moriah.

Abraham thought it all his
faith. As usual, Sarah didn't
let on.

## Advent in San Antonio

The college choir in Oregon rehearses
Christmas carols
in October, abetting
anticipation.

I remember.

Advents don't march
toward us.
They await
our kneeling,
ever bent toward
the little town.

I remember.

The oddness of the city
lit up with luminarias
made by old Hispanic women
who walk along the river placing
brown bags of sand and candles,
against the concrete of
the river bank
where Santa arrives floating
on a boat down the river,
waving his arm to children
who've never seen
snow.

I remember.

It's not so odd, for
they knelt to the
advent too
as it comes,
wooing us
all to
kneel,
waiting hope that
changes
tomorrow
and points us toward
the little town.

# How Old Was My Granddad?

*In memory of my
mother's father, Elgin
and for my son, Micah*

Granddad was old
when I was six.
Fifty-four,
to be exact.

I tell my six-year old son
about the old days or,
as he says, when asking
"Tell me about when you were little."

The stories spill out
like sap from the buckets we boys carried
at maple-sugar time,
going to Grannie and Granddad's
over Easter break,
hauling up buckets of
clear nectar
turning to amber,
liquid sugar
when granddad came home
from the dirt and grime of Long's
foundry to make magic with the
oak fire under long,
low pans.

Not enough trees
for anything commercial
but plenty to make it seem a
huge operation
for a seven and a nine
year old, my younger
brother and me.

The stories spill out
 like milk into the bucket at
the am/pm collection,
a far cry from buying
milk at am/pm corner markets
ubiquitous in the various cities
where I've lived.

The cows he milked
were fed from his
half-acre pasture and
up the road at a
neighbor's. And in the winter,
hay. Once he tried to teach me the
art of building a hay
stack. I wished I'd paid
closer attention.

The stories spill out
Like eggs from the chickens
my grandparents gathered each day
and sold to family and friends.

My son knows the sound now,
our neighbor's chickens clucking to lay
each morning while he and I sit to read
at six or seven while

mom catches a few more
winks.

His imagination spills out,
seeing my Granddad
ancient, like the old-timey
tools we see at
antique shops we
sometimes frequent.

Or maybe even older,
like the redwoods we've
seen only in picture
books.

Not all the stories
spill out.
I haven't the heart
to tell my son
that I am older now
than my grandfather was
when I was six and these
stories were first
made
to live.

My granddad wasn't
old, but I sure feel
like I am.

Granddad would've had a
chuckle
over that.

# A Plant Too Quick

*For Micah and Susan*

Let no water touch
this boy who balks at shampoo,
baths and soap. Only let him
play, alone, one hour more
amidst the cauliflowers and beans that
just last week poked their heads above the
mulch and dirt in which my gardening son
dreams.

He waters plants with
abandon, getting soaked and covered
over with mud.

Give him a shower
 with sprinkler heads,
although I fear the water will
grow him too much like a radish—so
quick its hard to believe it's ready to
harvest.

Let's make-believe instead
that I will ever keep this memory as a
fountain of his
youth.

# Ludwig's Language Games

*For Micah who will someday understand*

1.0        Imagine a tribe
    whose language
left out
the
      metaphor,
      the
          figure,
          the
              imagination.

1.1        Suppose an outsider said
    an untruth then
laughed about the
      bluff.
      The
          tribe wouldn't get
          the
              joke.

1.2        Language games.
     Look and see.
Meaning is use.
      Famous lines
      from
          Wittgenstein.

2.0        Ludwig

   had Asperger's.
Maybe.
   Why else would
    he move from
     picture theory to
      language games,
       unless he finally
        understood
   himself:
an outsider to other people's
   form of life.

3.0     To doubt Ludwig's language games
   is to fail to see,
  to listen,
 to hear.
To fail to "look and see"
  my son who
   often doesn't get
  the
   joke.

4.0 One doesn't have to imagine the tribe.

5.0 Whereof one cannot speak, thereof one must be silent.

5.1 Should we urge the tribe to speak?
  Our language?

5.2 Or listen to its silence?
  its meditation on the world?

5.3 A world without metaphor, without figure, without imagination might just be

5.4 the real world.

6.0 It might, in fact, just be a world where God is more
      concrete than all our theology
          allows; a total incarnation of God's
              presence.

7.0       The Lord is in his holy temple;
            let all the earth be
              silent before him.

# The Anti-Hum Society

Since Micah was about 2 or so, he has refused to let me hum. Never. Not a thing. Not even a happy song. For someone who has hummed, to myself I thought, all my life, not humming is more challenging than not eating that slice of rich chocolate cake.

The sound of the hum, I suppose, is too much stimulation. Micah is very aware of his environment, noticing all sorts of things the rest of us pass by. Since he absorbs so much of what's going on around him, sorting out—and perhaps keeping out—certain sounds can be a challenge. Now he is five and a half and incredibly articulate. He loves words and the way they sound and he . . . hums. Well, he sings and hums, often at the top of his lungs. It's a long story.

Micah is no lover of hopping from one theme to another, at least in the big picture. When he sets his mind to enjoy something, there are very, very few limitations. When he was still three, our vacuum cleaner broke down. To be as precise as I can, the machine wouldn't turn on. It turned out that the cord rewind was jamming the switch somehow—who knew that such a thing was possible? The vacuum was, in fact, still is, a Sanyo with two big fat wheels and a little caster wheel under the front. The reader might wonder at the "still is" part of that last sentence. After all, if the machine won't turn on, why keep it? Well, we took it to the only vacuum place we were aware of, a small, locally owned shop. It's a store where a person can buy fabric, notions, dress patterns, sewing machines and, of course, vacuums—high-end vacuums, some costing over a thousand dollars! Who had any concept that a mere vacuum could bring such a high price? My idea of buying a vacuum (the once or twice I have) was the Red Dot, or the Big K or Lowe's—rather lowbrow sources. But then, I only knew of the small, locally owned shop because of their cloth. Little stores specializing in thousand-dollar vacuums were definitely not on my radar. But we wanted a repair, not to buy a new machine, and we found out that the small, locally owned shop, besides being a purveyor of cloth, sold and repaired vacuums. So off we went.

Once in the store, Micah made a beeline for the vacuums, his eyes lighting up like most kid's eyes do when they get into the toy isle. He never cared for most toys—the things that light up, and buzz and boom or dolls that smile, frown, pee, poop and pull their pants down to do it. Vacuums were another thing. He wanted us to get down every single vacuum off the rack and let him move it across the floor, happily vacuuming up the "sample dirt" (again, who knew vacuum salespeople had such things?). But after a try or two, he didn't want to turn them on. Too much noise—a hum, if you will. But he would merrily provide his own sound-effects to attend the imaginary dirt his turbo-powered, bagless, triple-filtered machine was sucking up from little squares of tile and carpet labeled with names like Miele, Sebo, and Orek. Ever after—or so it seemed to his parents—Micah wanted to watch videos of vacuum salespersons comparing vacuums. Who knew that if one wanted to spend hours online, there were an equal number of hours of YouTube videos of kids with vacuums, cats with vacuums, dogs with vacuums and, well, you get the picture or you can if you google it.

Sadly, after three visits (not in the same week, by any means) to the little, locally owned shop, we were asked not to return unless we were actually going to buy a vacuum. This was not a command from the very nice vacuum people but some mysterious owner-on-high type who obviously has no children. Not to be deterred, we went to the Red Dot, the Big K, Lowe's and other big box stores where little boys and their fascination with vacuums seemed welcomed. Or perhaps at least ignored. No one seemed to mind us getting down vacuum after vacuum to let Micah enjoy his passion. Of course, none of these vacuums cost more than a mere five hundred dollars. But best of all was the local Stark's Vacuum where Micah was befriended by the sales staff and welcomed to come as often as he wanted. Stark's is a vacuum heaven for a 4-year old!

They even let him come into the back and watch the technicians repair vacuums!! And at the downtown Portland store, they have a vacuum museum! Wow! Who knew? We do now and we now know more about vacuum cleaners than I ever thought there was to know. We are also the proud owners of a Miele, one of the line of thousand dollar plus vacuums (although we bought the very cheapest, three hundred dollar one)! I won't mention the birthday Micah received a vacuum cleaner as a gift or the collection of vintage and not so vintage vacuums in our garage (sometimes our spare room), mostly given to us or bought for a dollar or two at yard sales. Did you know that some antique vacuums have sold for as much as $10,000.00? That explains why the Sanyo "still is" in our possession, although in many pieces as it's become our experiment repair vacuum. None of us has ever figured out how to remove the cord return to fix the vacuum. Although the little locally owned shop people knew how to get it into pieces, they couldn't get the parts and no one at our house can figure out how to remove the wheels behind which resides the mysterious cord rewind. But we still own it!

The point is, Micah is passionate about his passions! Once he wants to understand and experience something, there's little that will deter him. But he is equally passionate about his anti-passions. Humming. Not allowed. Nothing. Not even a happy song. No music either. Not a radio, not a CD, not even an "old-timey" (as he would call it) vinyl record!

No music? None? Nope. Or very, very little (I'm prone to exaggeration). We could make tapes for him (I wouldn't have a clue how to burn a CD) with a selection of songs to his liking, mostly upbeat and almost always wordless. Except for a few Raffi songs, which seem OK. Many other songs are just too sad. And then there was a stretch of time that we had the words to Jimmy Buffet's "Margaritaville" memorized, along with a bevy of songs from the 50s, 60s and 70s. But then Micah started to understand the words and we thought too much romance might not be good for a two-year old. So our house was filled for a number of years with household sounds but nearly no music .

Until about seven months ago. Around Christmas, Susan ordered a *Mannheim Steamroller Christmas* CD and Micah loved many parts of it—all instrumental. So one day Susan ordered another CD—the *Young Person's Guide to the Orchestra*. She has terrific intuitions about what is right and good for Micah. And so we played the CD with him one night instead of reading as we sat on the bed. He loved it! (Or parts of it—some music is still too sad and he can tell in a couple of bars whether it will make him sad, so he tells us to "skip that one.") There is something about Henry Purcell's recurring theme that moves Micah deeply. When the instruments were played individually, Micah was right up there with the cherubs! For the last seven months in the evenings or while he played or when we were in the car we have listened to Hayden, Beethoven, Bach, Mozart and Tchaikovsky. And he really listens. You can see his brain taking in the strains of the violins, hearing the timpani beat, or catching the oboe or French horn playing the backdrop to the melody. We've read dozens of books about orchestras and all the instruments and their histories. The oboe comes to us from the shawm, the flute was keyed by Boehm in the 1700s to make it easier to play, the oldest organs were powered by water under the influence of some enormously creative ancient Greek musician. You can make idiophonic music with two stones and woodwinds really are made of wood, or were originally, and the brass is still made of brass (except sometimes of fiberglass!). And so on, and on, and on. I now know more about musical instruments, their sounds, and how they are made than I ever thought I'd know. Yesterday I had to turn off the CD so Micah would be able to concentrate on the puzzle we were putting together, otherwise he was mentally off marching to the beat of Purcell and friends.

We started Micah on piano a couple of months ago, and he has the rhythm native to Buddy Rich. He stands for hours, sometimes, a day and plucks out tunes (or tries) on the instruments we have. Music is a passion. Its roots, I think, go back to swinging—well, and maybe Jimmy Buffet's "Hamburger in Paradise." When he was about two, we put a swing on our back porch and Micah would swing and sing, especially about our then neighbor's dog whose name was Psyche. I would push Micah on the swing and he would sing out "Boof goes Psyche." While I'm not sure about the "boof" I am sure about his love for dogs, another passion, but, for our story, a bit of a rabbit trail. Of course, if you are a hound, what could be more interesting than a rabbit's trail?

But I digress. Somewhere along the way, Micah started to hum and sing, sometimes with words but more often now with strains of Beethoven's "Fifth" or Mozart's "Eine Kliene Nacht Music." Or perhaps the "Dance of the Sugar Plum Fairy." As I write this, Micah is humming along to moving cars while we listen to Hayden's chamber music. The hum in the background sounds a lot like the strains of this particular movement!

Why, then, does Micah not permit me to hum? I'm not sure, beyond what I've already said. It's too much, a sort of sensory overload when it comes from someone other than himself. So one day a few weeks ago, after once again being told not to hum, I asked Micah if he were a member of the Anti-Hum Society. He smiled, and then giggled with delight at these words. "Yes, I am," said he. And we joked about that for a few days. After a week or so, Micah changed the name to "The Anti-Hum and Trust Society." While I wanted to call it "The Anti-Hum Trust and Society," Micah insists that that is wrong. I've wondered if he just doesn't know what "Trust" means. But then I realized, perhaps the anti-hum and trust do go together because he has to trust me not to hum. Hmmmm?

Lest you think there is no such society, let me tell you that the society, although largely unknown, is bigger than you think. Just last week at the Portland Children's Museum the three of us sat across from a mom (or maybe a grandmom—being an older father, I'm careful not to make the mistake of many and assume parentage details) and her son. She was humming along with the music (some chestnut from the 1970s that I, personally, know well too). Her son says "stop humming!" She smiled and kept right on going, mumbling something about liking the song. I made a comment about our son not liking me to hum. She laughed and said she takes her son's comments as an invitation to hum and sing some more.

Not at our house. Our son could be the president of the Anti-Hum Society. Maybe he is. But after attending three car shows this summer, Micah's new interest is in everything cars (not trains, not planes, not boats—cars). Guess what? Did you know that cars hum when they move? And who knew that there is a car named a "Hummer?"

# Christological Hand Flappings: On Being an Autistic Child with Autism

*The* question is: Is this an autistic child or a child with autism? (Do we celebrate this child's being what she is or separate the way he is from what he is?) Perhaps we should ask the model child. Imagine Jesus, God's fullness among us, not being able to speak. (He couldn't, of course. At first the Word was speechless, like the rest of us.)

That's autism. Or imagine Jesus, God's fullness among us, concentrating only on lining up his toy cars or (worse!) playing only with the wheels. (He did single-mindedly aim at the cross. Makes you wonder why he spent so much time with wood growing up.)

That's autism. Imagine Jesus with no (so-called) "theory of mind." He did see everyone as an extension of himself. (We are the body of Christ.)

That's autism. Some might say Jesus used too many metaphors to be autistic. Maybe his use of metaphor makes the rest of us literalists. (Remember Nicodemus—how can I enter my mother's womb again?) Or is the world metaphorical at its core and Jesus just literal about it?

That's autism. Maybe we shouldn't try to answer *the* question, split the difference and say: This child is an autistic child with autism. Philosophically unclear, unspecified. But true to the autistic life with autism. (Is Jesus more clear when he says the least of these is greatest, or if you give a cold cup of water to the least of these, you give it to me?)

That's autism. The very things I love about my autistic child with autism are autistic things he does: His deep sense of anxiety (not just empathy but fear) for the homeless man panhandling by the freeway exit because that could happen to my son (do unto to others as you want them to do to you). If he lost those fears, his deep identification with others, would he change so much he'd no longer be himself? I wonder, did Jesus fear for us/his Body as my son fears for others/himself?

That's autism. Some autistic children with autism write but cannot speak. In writing they tell us that flapping their hands or running their fingers over and over through water is their way of communicating; their native tongue; their way of having the world communicate with them.

That's autism. When Jesus created the world, did he speak an oral language (and which one was it?) or did he flap his hands like a mother hen flaps her wings drawing the world together, or did he run his fingers through the water to separate land from sea?

That's autism. Some autistic children with autism see everything as alive. Is this a mistake or just a failure in everyone else's imagination? Jesus saw everything alive. (The very stones will cry out *Hosanna*)

That's autism. Some autistic children with autism know every emotion in the room (don't see how they do that with no theory of mind but they do). Jesus seems to know everyone's emotions too. (Consider the woman at the well, Pilate, the centurion or any of dozens of others.)

That's autism. One father of an autistic child with autism says autism is best understood as social construct and not realistically. A philosopher's point—turns out, many philosophers have autistic children with autism. Jesus makes us and maybe even the whole world as a social construct, spun out of his relationship with the other two divine persons. That makes us no less real.

That's autism. Maybe the new literal is just the old metaphor and heaven is a fully embodied way of being with others, the body of Christ, flapping our corporate hands and running our corporate fingers through water, caressing it with our love, God's love we have borrowed. *The* question is: Is this child an autistic child or a child with autism?

Is that a literal question?

www.ingramcontent.com/pod-product-compliance
Lightning Source LLC
Chambersburg PA
CBHW072010090426
42734CB00033B/2348